The Secret Plan

By

D. Sterling Harlow

XULON PRESS

The Secret Plan
Had he only known
by D. Sterling Harlow

Printed in the United States of America

ISBN 9781619049444

www.xulonpress.com

Table of Contents

Dedication

To my wonderful wife Marlene. Your love for all these years has given me the freedom to grow and write. Thank you so very much.

Introduction

What a joy it has been to write this book. Short, and to the point, it's one that every Christian should have and one everyone on earth should experience. It is my hope that each of you will learn the simple truths that lie within.

Forward

This morning, as I was listening to the radio, I heard the song "The Old Rugged Cross" and thoughts of my childhood came sweeping back to me. I don't remember exactly, but it was either this song or "Jesus Loves Me," that were the first Christian songs I learned as a little boy in church. Whatever the case, I know that those old songs had an effect on my life. I guess it is what God had in mind with the Old Testament. It was designed to be a keeper of souls until the advent of Christ. I know for my own life He used those songs to sow into me the truth that God is real. It didn't keep me from sinning, but it more than likely kept me alive. I think about all the times His face came to me when I was in the midst of trouble. Many times on board ship, during the long flight hours of Vietnam, His face, or just the knowledge of His reality, kept me from certain death.

In saying this, I want you to hear my heart. I have spent many hours, and much time thinking of the cross, and, as important as it is (we owe everything to what happened there), I know for me I can't stay there. Just as I had to go forward from the knowledge of God into a relationship with Him, you and I must move forward with the foundation of the cross beneath our feet, planted on that firm foundation. We must understand that the cross was a gate, a door that has been opened for us to the high calling of God and what He has planned for each one of us.

Without this foundation, it is easy to get lost in all the who, the what, the why, and the where of our walk with Jesus.

We must make the decision to enter in through this gate and push on to becoming all that God had in mind for us when He made us. This door leads us to a highway full of rich rewards which are waiting for us just beyond the next bend in this road of life. Hopefully, this little book will remind us of all of the treasures that this relationship with Him holds in store.

Duane Harlow

1

God's Awesome Secret Plan

D o you believe it would be possible for a man, to create
a situation where all those people he grew up with,
his good friends, and his family, would turn against him and
reject him? After which he would be ridiculed and then be
beaten by some of those very men, whipped to the bone and
nailed up on a tree for all to see. Yet, this is what our Lord
chose to go through for us. Not only did He choose this sce-
nario, He planned, it and said He was looking forward to it.
This is in part the new covenant that He longed to shared
with His disciples on the day we now call the last supper.
In reality it was the last Passover Seder He would have with
them.

   No matter what it sounds like, this was not the plan of
a mad man. No, it was a very carefully choreographed plan
which was created before time came into being. The Creator
of all, the God of all creation, conceived this plan at the same
time He was making plans for the creation of you and me.
Before the Earth was made, He planned His own death on
the cross as a counter plan for all the sin that He knew would
take place throughout the age of time on this world.

This same sin would be responsible for the separation between God and you and I, his creation. It was in fact a secret master plan, to restore mankind and his Creator back into the relationship they shared in the beginning. And guess who fell right into it? That's right, satan. (I will not capitalize his name) That's why it had to be a secret plan so when it happened, satan would think he was winning. Yet, all the while we, you and I, would become the beneficiaries of this clandestine ambush of the enemy. We would be set free from sin and its guilt and shame once and for all and be once more free from the enemy of our souls.

For all we know, the Word of God who became Jesus the Christ had never been separated from the Father or eternity before He allowed Himself to be found as a human, a created human who lived in the world of time. Before time was, He had spent eternity on His throne in the heavenly places. Now, this Word of God became flesh for us and the son of man to carry out the plan of plans. He, Himself, would become the payment for all sin, for all time, so we could once again live with the Father when time is no more. We understand that time was created for us but in heaven time is not.

So much had to be given up by this Word. He reigned in Glory and then found Himself on earth as a man, in a world polluted by sin. His glorious creation, you and me, rotting away, eaten up with the thoughts of men instead of the thoughts of God. What a cost! What unbelievable pain He must have felt and it was all for us. It's no wonder Jesus wept when He saw His city Jerusalem enveloped in the darkness of religion. Here He finds Himself in the thick of the war of wars, not as a warrior clad with fine armor, but a lamb to be sacrificed. One could ask, "Is this anyway to fight a war?" The right response is yes, with a lamb!

What was all this for? Why did He do this? John 17 tells us why. (*[20] My prayer is not for them alone. I pray also for those who will believe in me through their message, [21] that all of them may be one, Father, just as you are in me and I am in you. May they also be in us so that the world may believe that you have sent me. [22] I have given them the glory that you gave me, that they may be one as we are one: [23] I in them and you in me. May they be brought to complete unity to let the world know that you sent me and have loved them even as you have loved me. [24] Father, I want those you have given me to be with me where I am, and to see my glory, the glory you have given me because you loved me before the creation of the world. [25] Righteous Father, though the world does not know you, I know you, and they know that you have sent me. [26] I have made you known to them, and will continue to make you known in order that the love you have for me may be in them and that I myself may be in them.)* Again I ask; Why? So *we* could once again be one with Jesus and be one with the Father.

We are not a mere reflection of the Lord's Glory, although that would have been awesome if that was all there was for us. We have been given the same glory that the Father gave Jesus. What a wonderful gift! We were called to be His glorious representations on this Earth, not just a reflection, but also the image of Him who gave Himself for us. The image of Him who was poured out for the sin of all men. The image of Him who gave up heaven for us, so we could once again stand in the Glory of Him who gave glory its meaning.

What are we doing with such a wonderful gift? Do we use it to usher in the glory of God? What have we done? What have we done with the gift of this glory? Could it be that this gift, this marvelous gift, has been covered over with our soiled souls? Have we been covered over with dross, and is this awesome work that He is doing in us the skimming away of all of these impurities to bring out the gold, our true color so it could show through to the world?

We have just received a word here in our home church from a very well known prophet, who said the glory of God had departed from our city for a season but now that precious glory has once again returned.

We have spent many months warring for our city and our nation, and, now, with the blessing of the presence of the Spirit of God once more in our midst, we are truly looking forward to our future. We have been given this wonderful word as a gift, and it was given on Father's Day. The Father of us all gave us a Father's Day present.

Of course all this had to be proceeded by Calvary.

What Have I Learned

_____

_____

_____

_____

_____

_____

_____

_____

_____

_____

_____

_____

_____

_____

_____

_____

_____

_____

_____

_____

_____

_____

_____

_____

_____

_____

_____

2

Raised to be Slaughtered

The Lord has been showing me that the cross means so much more than just our salvation. Praise God, it does mean that! Jesus did die on the cross for our eternal existence with Him. But the cross is much more than that. The cross is a door to the sin of mankind, a door which Jesus blew away with His blood. This door was the only thing holding us back, blocking us from being in right relationship with our creator. Jesus had to take our sin and it had to be nailed to this door and, once it was, it was blown away forever, and sin was completely paid for.

When this took place, two things happened. We were now declared holy and righteous in the sight of God, so now we could enter into the Holy presence of our heavenly Father. And we were now able to receive from this Holy Creator of all things, His love, His care and His anointing, like that which comes from a true father.

Sin had kept us out of His presence so He, Himself, made a way to be reunited, reconciled with His creations, His sons and His daughters. He came down as God-man and He allowed Himself to become the blood sacrifice for all mankind. Man was now able to touch Him and to be touched by Him. This was a deliberate act of love by the One who made us and gave us life, but now He gave us true life. His goal of being able to relate again with us as in the beginning was now accomplished.

It had taken at least seven thousand years to bring this event to Earth. Even for God this must have been a long time, or then again, maybe with Him it was just one day. Many times in the past He had come and blessed us with His presence, but He could never truly relate with us as a Father and hold us in His arms and comfort us. His Holy presence would have destroyed us.

Obviously, the cross of Christ or that piece of wood was not the real door, but it was Jesus who hung upon it which was the real door to life and forgiveness for us all.

When Jesus died on that cross, His heavenly Father tore His robe in the same way the high priest would tear his robe when a blasphemy would take place in his presence. The earthly expression of this was the tearing of the curtain in the Temple. That curtain had kept us separate from the Holy of Holies and relationship with the Father. This curtain was torn in two from top to bottom as a man would tear his clothes. By this act He made access for us, to restoration and relation-ship with Him. And at the same time, it spoke of the great blasphemy that had just taken place. God, the Son, had just died, full of all the judgments that were against held against us in the courts of heaven. This of course included all sin the of mankind. That curtain had been a safety shield for us and because of this, the tearing away of it, you and I are now free to go out and represent Him. We have the privilege of going everywhere in this world and inviting others to come into the Holy of Holies along with us to meet their Creator. We get the right to introduce the lost to their savior.

One but has to look at the massive heavens above or the Earth and all it contains, and you may ask why? Why would the creator of all of this humble Himself and come down (Emmanuel, God with us) and die as a man, as one of His own creations? Why? Because He made us to represent Him and to have relationship with Him! We are His workmanship, created in His image and likeness and He wanted us back.

Jesus Christ is the stone on which the Word of God was written, the unchangeable Word and He then left up to you and I as individuals as to how it was to be applied. It came with authority, but it was motivated by love. This love saw the Creator of all things (whether things on earth or things in heaven, things with breath, or things established without breath, the one who created everything that was created) hung on a tree for our sins so you and I could be free, free to be in right relationship with Him who died and rose again.

Have you ever wondered why the Bible says in I Corinthians 11:24 that Jesus Himself says, "This is my body which is broken for you," (KJV or Amp.) and yet it also says, "not one of His bones were broken"? This, without understanding, can be troublesome.

Now, if you can handle this, Jesus was the stone the Ten Commandments were written on. It was a shadow of His death, burial and resurrection. Jesus was the Word of God, written on the stone tablets. These were then broken when Moses got mad at what he saw the people doing when he came down from the mountain. The people had made another God, a golden calf, because they believed Moses had died on the mountain. So Moses threw them down and destroyed them and a new set of tablets had to be made. The first set was made by God, but the second set God made Moses chisel out. Sounds like the Garden of Eden all over again. God's way or our way? We see this picture played out so many times in Scripture. Jericho was God's way, and Ai was man's way. Crucifixion or King? God's way or man's way. Of course now on this side of the cross the words are written on the tablet of our hearts. He has not given us hearts of stone but rather hearts of flesh which can be molded by Him.

After this picture of the cross, David writes Psalm 22. This is a very graphic narrative of Jesus dying on the cross.

[2] O my God, I cry out by day, but you do not answer, by night, and am not silent. [3]Yet you are enthroned as the Holy One; you are the praise of Israel. [4] In you our fathers put their trust; they trusted and you delivered them. [5] They cried to you and were saved; in you they trusted and were not disappointed. [6]But I am a worm and not a man, scorned by men and despised by the people. [7] All who see me mock me; they hurl insults, shaking their heads: [8] He trusts in the LORD; let the LORD rescue him. Let him deliver him, since he delights in him. [9]Yet you brought me out of the womb; you made me trust in you even at my mother's breast. [10] From birth I was cast upon you; from my mother's womb you have been my God. [11] Do not be far from me, for trouble is near and there is no-one to help. [12]Many bulls surround me; strong bulls of Bashan encircle me. [13] Roaring lions tearing their prey open their mouths wide against me. [14] I am poured out like water, and all my bones are out of joint. My heart has turned to wax; it has melted away within me. [15] My strength is dried up like a potsherd, and my tongue sticks to the roof of my mouth; you lay me in the dust of death. [16] Dogs have surrounded me; a band of evil men has encircled me, they have pierced my hands and my feet. [17] I can count all my bones; people stare and gloat over me. [18] They divide my garments among them and cast lots for my clothing.

So there is no doubt that Jesus and the cross were always a part of the equation in God' plan for mankind to be created. Never doubt what God has planned for all our tomorrows, and remember this, He is never late with His plans.

Some of you will have trouble with what I am going to say next. The book of Hebrews tells us in chapters 9 and 10 that forgiveness of our sins is eternal. The Word of God, or the Bible as we call it, also tells us that we cannot crucify Jesus again and again. He died on the cross once and for all. The blood covered all sin forever and for all mankind. Because God had commanded a blood Sacrifice for sin it is quite clear that Jesus was the Lamb of God and it was His blood which took away the sin of the world.

It doesn't say that we will never sin again once we have been converted. We will, and we do sin all the time. But the penalty for this sin has all been paid for in full.

I John 2:1 tells us that if we do sin we have an advocate, Jesus, the Christ, with the Father who comes between judgment and us. *¹ My dear children, I write this to you so that you will not sin. But if anybody does sin, we have one who speaks to the Father in our defense— Jesus Christ, the Righteous One.* He intercedes for us with the Father. It's a done deal. Repentance after conversion is only a religious exercise if, when doing so, it means reapplying the blood of Christ over and over again. He only died once for us, but that is all it took. Repentance is a key part of our walk with Jesus, but it should never be used by the church or anyone else to bring guilt or condemnation. The thinking here is that if we can be kept guilty about our sins, then we won't sin as often. This is not biblical. Repentance is not turn or burn as we have been taught. It does mean to stop doing whatever you were doing that is not pleasing to God, and the idea is to then move closer to living for Christ. The church has also used this forever to keep us in control. Yet the very Word of God says: *"It's the goodness of God that leads us to repentance".*

When Jesus said on the cross, "It is finished," it truly was. He did it all. Does this give us license to sin? Not if we are truly saved. The conviction of the Holy Spirit is what keeps us from wanting to sin. But the good news is that God has already covered us if and when we do. It remains only for us to ask to be forgiven. This is grace, and it came way before the foundation of the world.

For centuries, if we wanted complete forgiveness, we (the church) would make people jump through all kinds of hoops. When is forgiveness not forgiveness? When what Jesus did on the cross is not enough! We could not be restored back into relationship with the Father and still be guilty of sin. It simply can not be.

Yes, we should try to be better. But this is for us so we can enjoy all God has for us but it is not for our salvation. We can work on those things that we know are not right in us, and, if we want to refer to this as repentance, that's ok. There is healing for all of this, but the sin and judgment of these things has already been paid for, and we cannot pay for it again. We have been bought (purchased with a price) and paid for. We, who are in Christ Jesus, do not belong to ourselves. We belong to Him.

I am not saying that there is no consequence for sin in this world. You commit a murder or robbery or break the law of this land and if you get caught, you will go to jail or have to pay some fine. We are still in this world, but not of this world. We must pay the world what we owe it, but Jesus already paid the ultimate price for our sins and we can't.

New International Version - UK (NIVUK)

[19] Show me the coin used for paying the tax. They brought him a denarius, [20] and he asked them, Whose portrait is this? And whose inscription? [21] Caesar's, they replied. Then he said to them, Give to Caesar what is Caesar's, and to God what is God's. Matthew 22:19-22

[1]Therefore let us leave the elementary teachings about Christ and go on to maturity, not laying again the foundation of repentance from acts that lead to death, and of faith in God, [2]instruction about baptisms, the laying on of hands, the resurrection of the dead, and eternal judgment. [3]And God permitting, we will do so. (Hebrews 6:1-3)

We as the church still have much to learn.

What Have I Learned

_____

_____

_____

_____

_____

_____

_____

_____

_____

_____

_____

_____

_____

_____

_____

_____

_____

_____

_____

_____

_____

_____

_____

3

Immanuel

I have never been able to get past Isaiah 7:14, which says, *"Therefore the Lord himself will give you a sign: The virgin will be with child and will give birth to a son, and will call him Immanuel."* And Matthew 1:20-23, *"But after he had considered this, an angel of the Lord appeared to him in a dream and said, "Joseph son of David, do not be afraid to take Mary home as your wife, because what is conceived in her is from the Holy Spirit. She will give birth to a son, and you are to give him the name Jesus, because he will save his people from their sins." All this took place to fulfill what the Lord had said through the prophet: "The virgin will be with child and will give birth to a son, and they will call him Immanuel"—which means, "God with us." Jesus was His name, Immanuel is who He is!*

This signifies a full circle of events. God made us to relate with Him. (Genesis 1:26-27) His desire was to have a man created in His own likeness to be able to relate with. This was the purpose in our creation. We were designed for fellowship with God which is what we had with Him in the garden in the beginning and what we now have through the blood of Christ available to us once again.

When we fell God waited for sin to have its reign, and then after five thousand years, (#5 means grace) He gave us Immanuel. He would, as in the beginning, be able to relate face to face with His creation without destroying us with His righteousness and unapproachable light. It has been approximately seven thousand years, (#7 means complete,) and I am wondering what's next? Do we have another thousand years which would make eight, (#8 means new-beginnings) or is time almost over, and the last thousand years could be the thousand-year reign with Him? I do know one thing, I want to be ready, and not caught without oil for my lamp. Not even the Son knows the time the Father has set for His return.

Others believe it has only been six thousand years. But with six, meaning man, which would then mean the year of man, with seven meaning completion, both of these cry out to me "get ready," I'm coming back soon.

When I think about this, and then look at myself, that gets a bit scary. However, this is what transformation is all about, being restored to what we were like before the fall. *"And we, who with unveiled faces all reflect the Lord's glory, are being transformed into his likeness with ever-increasing glory, which comes from the Lord, who is the Spirit." (II Corinthians 3:18)* OK, I feel better. I can live with that. I am being restored. This process goes on and on and on until He comes for me. His word Awesome! says, *"that He will be faithful to complete that which He began in us." (Philippians 1:6)*

"For God so loved the world that He gave His only begotten Son that who-so-ever believes in Him will not parish but will have ever-lasting life." (John 3:16)

What happened to us when man fell in the garden was not pretty. We voluntarily sold ourselves into slavery to the ruler of this world. The cross bought us back. Jesus paid the ransom price in full, but we act as if it never happened. We are still serving another god (as if there really is another God). This one has our name on it. It's called self-centeredness. We took on the very costly covenant of the enemy, that which only knows how to kill, steal, and destroy, in place of the covenant of God's love. Again we see the 10 commandments vs the golden calf.

What Have I Learned

_____

_____

_____

_____

_____

_____

_____

_____

_____

_____

_____

_____

_____

_____

_____

_____

_____

_____

_____

_____

_____

_____

_____

4

We Belong to Him

Listen to the cry in James' voice as he writes and I'm going to paraphrase this: "You still don't get it! You still believe (after all Jesus has done for you) that this life is all about you and *Santa* Jesus." We want what we want no matter what the Lord wants for us and, when He doesn't give it to us, we get angry with Him. We fight, kick and scream to get our way and then turn our back on Him when He suggests that there might be a better way. We ask, but what we want is all about what we think we need, and the very thing we want, may be the worst choice we could make.

He paid for us and we belong to Him. Oh yeah, I can hear the voice crying out, "I don't belong to anyone. I'm my own person." Well, let me tell you, that's the main problem. You see, it all belongs to God and no matter how hard we fight to gain control, we can't change that fact. The Earth and all that is on it belongs to Him. He made it all and He made it for Himself.

¹The earth is the LORD's, and everything in it, the world, and all who live in it; ² for he founded it upon the seas and established it upon the waters. (Psalm 24) He planned it for our good. He had us in mind when He created it all, but it all came from Him and it's His! That's why James says that our God is a jealous God. He is the lover of our souls and He wants desperately to have relationship with us. I say desperately because of His plan to buy us back. It cost Him His only Son. I would call that desperate, wouldn't you? It also gives us a hint of our value to Him.

If we want to try to buy our lives back from God, just keep walking on that fence that separates the world's ways from God's ways. And, sooner or later we will give ourselves back to the enemy. We have the right to make that choice, but we can never stop being loved by Jesus. However, we can keep ourselves from taking full advantage of living under His rule and authority within His kingdom. We can keep ourselves out of the enjoyment of living in the fullness of His kingdom here on earth and from under His covering and blessings and in the kingdom to come. All we have to do is keep wanting our own way rather than His.

Do you remember the story of the prodigal son? He got his way, and when that turned out to be ugly and not at all what he dreamt it would be, he turned around and came back to the Father's house then the story gets good again. The blesses his returned son and treats him as if he never left.

The Word of God says this, *"but each one is tempted when, by his own evil desire, he is dragged away and enticed. Then, after desire has conceived, it gives birth to sin; and sin, when it is full-grown, gives birth to death." (James 1:14-15) NIV*

Now let's read from James 4 together, *"What causes fights and quarrels among you? Don't they come from your desires that battle within you? You want something but don't get it. You kill and covet, but you cannot have what you want. You quarrel and fight. You do not have, because you do not ask God. When you ask, you do not receive, because you ask with wrong motives, that you may spend what you get on your pleasures. You adulterous people, don't you know that friendship with the world is hatred toward God? Anyone who chooses to be a friend of the world becomes an enemy of God. Or do you think Scripture says without reason that the Spirit He caused to live in us envies intensely? (Or that God jealously longs for the spirit that He made to live in us; or that the Spirit He caused to live in us longs jealously?) But He gives us more grace. That is why Scripture says: "God opposes the proud but gives grace to the humble." "Submit yourselves then, to God. Resist the devil, and he will flee from you. Come near to God and he will come near to you. Wash your hands, you sinners, and purify your hearts, you double-minded." (James 4:1-8) NIV* I have removed the verse numbers so it reads as written.

I recently received this e-mail. I think it speaks directly to this. Whomever the author of this is, thank you!

"A scientist says to God, 'We don't need you anymore. Science has finally figured out a way to create life out of nothing. In other words, we can now do what you did in the beginning. We can take dirt and form it into the likeness of You and breathe life into it, thus creating man' *'Well that's interesting '*, says God.' *Show Me.'* So the scientist bends down to the earth and starts to mold the soil. *'Oh, no, no, no,'*...interrupts God. (I love this) *"Get your own dirt!"*

The truth is, there is nothing, nothing at all that we can make or do, that does not involve the creation of God...... *"You are worthy, our Lord and God, to receive glory and honor and power, for you created all things, and by your will they were created and have their being." (Revelation 4:11)*

What Have I Learned

_____

_____

_____

_____

_____

_____

_____

_____

_____

_____

_____

_____

_____

_____

_____

_____

_____

_____

_____

_____

_____

_____

_____

5

Restored to Relationship

G od sent his Son to die on that tree for the expressed purpose of bringing us back to Him. *"For Christ died for sins once for all, the righteous for the unrighteous, to bring you to God." (I Peter 3:18)*

Again the Word says: *"but with the precious blood of Christ, a lamb without blemish or defect. He was chosen before the creation of the world, but was revealed in these last times for your sake." (1 Peter 1:19-20)* Before the world was created He was chosen to be the one to pay the price for sin for you and me. In the book of John it says, *"the Lamb of God who takes away the sin of the world."* Please take some time and think about each of those words. There is great freedom found here.

The result of this was so God could bless his creation once again. To be in the presence of God is to receive His blessings. Look what happened to Obed-Edom when David had to abandon his first attempt to bring the Ark of the Lord back to Jerusalem. David had to learn the power of the presence of God and the correct way to handle it. His way sounded great, but it wasn't God's way. *"The ark of the LORD remained in the house of Obed-Edom the Gittite for three months, and the LORD blessed him and his entire household." (2 Samuel 6:11)*

Do you think that Obed-Edom was more righteous than King David? Did the Lord come down and clean up Obed-Edom and his family before he blessed them? No! The presence of God is for the blessing of His creation.

This must have made quite an impression on Obed-Edom for he chose to go with the ark and to make his place as close to it as possible.

I don't know about you, but it has always puzzled me when I read the story of David trying to bring the Ark home to the temple in the non-prescribed way. David's heart was right but it still didn't go well. When Uzzah was killed while he tried to steady the Ark on the new cart, it seemed to me that this was not a fair way of handling the situation. God must have been mad at David and took it out on poor Uzzah. I have known for many years that God took out all His anger on Jesus at the cross. I'm not sure where I came up with this teaching, but it was from one of the churches I attended when I was young. It was just one of those things that I had set aside in my mind to find out the answer at a later time, like putting something away so good that you never can find it again on purpose. Then, all of a sudden, there it is. You find it while looking for something else. If you know me at all you would understand the problem I might have with this as I am a teacher of the love of God and the relationship He wants to have with us. With God, relationship is everything!

Well, the time came for the answer the other day while I was sitting in our church soaking up His presence and he gave me a new revelation on this.

Uzzah did not understand the awesome power in the presence of God. He handled the Ark as casually as one might handle any piece of furniture. This casual view of God cost him his life. The presence of God demands our awe and reverence, and we, in our world of grace, still don't understand this. The mercies of God are great and His love does cover a multitude of sins. We must continue to rely on the grace of God as we try to work out this relationship with our Lord. How easy it has become to treat the things of God with contempt. If it were not for grace, we would all be lost like poor Uzzah.

We are just learning the awesome magnitude of Your glory Lord. At the burning bush Moses had to remove his shoes as he stood in wonder before an image of Your glory. Oh God, thank you for Your grace. Help us learn of You more deeply. Help us drink of you more deeply.

The grace of God is not greasy but pure, as pure as everything else about Him. Lord God, thank You for being a never, ever changing God. You never change but You are ever changing us. Your grace is truly amazing. I am overwhelmed with the understanding of how I desperately need Your grace. Amen.

Truth is, I know that my position in Christ is secure but why do we live our lives that way? What I mean is this. We live our lives like we have a cheap gospel. We take advantage of the grace of God and His mercy on us.

The fact is, before the cross we would never have gotten away with this. God got angry with sin in man and those who said they believed, but lived as if He didn't exist.

This is what killed Uzzah. Uzzah lived like he was a believer but acted as if God were a tame God, and not the awesome God that destroyed nations. He had no reverential fear of the presence of God. The awareness of the awesomeness of God was lost, if it had ever been there to begin with.

Today most of us still live with a convenient, watered down gospel. We believe it has no teeth, or worse, that the teeth of the Lion of Judah are only for the enemy.

Yes, we live in grace on this side of the cross, and I am truly glad for this, but God hasn't changed. He is still the same today, yesterday and forever. He is still an awesome, mighty Holy God who deserves our highest praise and to be treated as Holy. Remember, grace was His idea. I am so glad I live on this side of the cross, aren't you?

Uzzah died from unbelief in who God truly was, and so will the many who choose not to trust in Jesus. He showed me that it was the pure power of His presence and His awesome Glory that killed Uzzah.

We've always read this story wrong. It's was not about David, it was about the awesomeness of our God. Not even the priest who carried the Ark could touch it. They had to carry it on two poles, one on each side, with four of them, two in front and two in the rear carrying it. When the Ark was in the Temple, the priest had to approach it carefully and in the prescribed way. There was always a genuine fear of God in the Holy of Holies. David had to learn to handle the presence of God in the prescribed way before he could bring the ark home.

Because our Father tore His robe, (the curtain in the Temple) and created access to His presence through Jesus on the cross, we can now touch and be touched by Him, without fear. The blood that the priest sprinkled made peace for one year but the blood of Christ Jesus made peace with God for you and me forever.

Had I known that I had the right to touch His presence, things might have been very different for my life. Many years ago when in the process of planting a new work in Northern California I had a visitation from God while in worhship. When the Ark came down in my living room some twenty years ago, as we were worshiping the Lord, I didn't have a clue what to do with it. My living room was where the church we were planting was meeting at the time. Because of that story of Uzzah and some teaching that had brought fear, teaching that I had heard so many years before, I was afraid to touch it, Instead of rejoicing in His presence, I was filled with fear, so in the spirit I covered it up with a sheet and soon He left. Thank you, Lord, that you are a God of second chances.

God has since healed the damage that this did so many years ago in my heart. We, as pastors, teachers and leaders, must be very careful what kind of impressions our teachings leave on peoples hearts, about our God. We can scar forever those we are called to love, bless, and teach about the goodness of our God.

Now that we have become the ark and the temple of God as He has chosen to live in us, how do we treat Him? Unfortunately for many, we treat Him as if it's no big deal. We've become so callused, so used to this fact, that we at times even forget He's around. Yet we know that He says, "I will never leave you nor forsake you."

He goes everywhere we go, even to those dark shady places that we sometimes visit when there's no one else around. He knows the thoughts and intentions of the heart, but we treat Him as if He is blind and has lost His hearing.

We must contend for new understandings about God. Fear His awesomeness, but don't be afraid of Him. If we are afraid of Him, then we won't draw near to Him, and we will miss the glory of relationship with our God.

When we finally get to the place where we understand the extent of the love relationship we have with the Father, it will change forever how we live our lives. Actually, we may even allow Him to take over the running of our lives, even though this is not His plan. He wants us to live our life as if for Him. To help with this process, guilt, fear, shame, unbelief and worry, were all nailed to the cross along with Jesus. What will we do when we learn to live without them?

I'm not sure but I am looking forward to the day when that happens. How about you?

These scriptures in Revelation are vital if we are to understand what our God has accomplished for us as a lion, as a lamb, as a man, and as God! *"Then I saw a Lamb, looking as if it had been slain, standing in the center of the throne, encircled by the four living creatures and the elders. He had seven horns and seven eyes, which are the seven spirits of God sent out into all the earth. He came and took the scroll from the right hand of him who sat on the throne. And when he had taken it, the four living creatures and the twenty-four elders fell down before the Lamb. Each one had a harp and they were holding golden bowls full of incense, which are the prayers of the saints. And they sang a new song: "You are worthy to take the scroll and to open its seals, because you were slain, and with your blood you purchased men for God from every tribe and language and people and nation. You have made them to be a kingdom and priests to serve our God, and they will reign on the earth." (Revelation 5:6-10)*

We serve a mighty and awesome God who was alive, who was dead, and now lives forevermore. This reminds me of a large sign that I had painted over the front door of my church in Ramona, California. It said, *"Jesus is Alive"*. It was during the years when the cool ones were saying, "God is dead." I've been in His tomb in Jerusalem, and He isn't there.

Isaiah, in Chapter 6 verses 1-5, when he got the vision of God, says this, *"In the year that King Uzziah died, I saw the Lord seated on a throne, high and exalted, and the train of his robe filled the temple. Above him were seraphs, each with six wings: With two wings they covered their faces, with two they covered their feet, and with two they were flying. And they were calling to one another: "Holy, holy, holy is the LORD Almighty; the whole earth is full of his glory." At the sound of their voices the doorposts and thresholds shook and the temple was filled with smoke. "Woe to me!" I cried. "I am ruined! For I am a man of unclean lips, and I live among a people of unclean lips, and my eyes have seen the King, the LORD Almighty."*

You and I are what I call the glory lamps of God which He is sending into the whole Earth. We are to go about igniting other glory lamps as we go. What a privilege to carry the glory of our Lord everywhere we go.

The glory and majesty of our God and King blew Isaiah away. He was never the same after his encounter with his Lord. He could never be the same after seeing the God of all creation, and this is the same God who desires desperately to have relationship with us. Wow!

I don't think many people understand the fullness of what is ours in relationship with Christ. Jesus is the first human being (fully human) to act out in the flesh what God created man for. I believe that there are fewer still who act out as Jesus did, and yet this is in our DNA. It's what we were made for!

Most people are just not aware of what being created in God's image means for us, and that we are called to embody God in us and then show it to all the world.

Understanding that Jesus acted as a man while He was on this Earth and showed all of us what was available to us through Him as His creations, has truly been slow in coming to my understanding. Yet as this enlightenment comes to us, how can we deny this calling? How can we not cloth ourselves in Christ Jesus and do the works created by God for us to walk in before He created the earth? Jesus showed us what acting like the image of God is supposed to look like. We've attributed it to the fully God part of Him and not the fully human part of God that He came to show us. With His help we can do it.

When Jesus walked around healing everyone He touched, it was for us. When Jesus walked around and was tempted by sin, it was for us. When He spoke the Word, it was for us. When He fulfilled the prophecies written about Him, it was for us. When He did creative miracles such as healing (example-this man was born blind), it was for us. When He walked in relationship with His Father in heaven and with the people on Earth, it was for us. When He gave Himself up on the cross for our sins, it was for us.

All these things Jesus did as a human being, it was for our benefit He did them. He was saying to the people then and now to us, "You go and do the same things and even more."

Jesus chose to live within the limits of His humanness, and yet when speaking with His disciples the Bible records this, *"If you have seen Me you have seen the Father."* Jesus is the exact expression of the Father, but He is not the Father. He is God and yet He is only part of God. The Father God is not Jesus, nor is He the Holy Spirit, yet they are one God. God is God and there is no other, yet there are three who make up that one glorious God, God the Father, God the Son, and God the Holy Spirit.

Even as I am writing this, I look at the tarnished image I portray of the awesome God and I ask myself this question: When are you, Duane, going to fully believe this? I know this is the truth and how we are to relate with this world, and yet I fail at it so miserably. I want to believe all of it, with no doubts and no unbelief, and yet when I look at myself, I cry out for mercy. How can this wonderful God expect me to do what Jesus did? Answer: Because He lives in me and it is not about me but about He who dwells in me His temple. He will do it through us.

Yet we go on learning. Twenty years ago what I now write would be called heresy, and in some circles it still might be. Not long ago people with this view could expect to be cast out of the church or worse, burned at the stake. What we should have learned from the first church just after the resurrection of Christ, we didn't keep. Somewhere man looked at man and saw weakness and lost sight of Jesus and the power of God in man.

Some are still there, but many have chosen to move forward with the on going revelation of God and search for the Christ in His creation. He is there. He lives in you and me and we must come to the understanding that this was His plan all along. He wants to work through us! Every one of us! We are to be His likeness to the world.

Jesus was and is a model for us, but not to pattern our lives as a reflection of His, but with all the individuality He made you and me to have. He gave me my own personality, my own understandings of Him, my own mind which is different from others, and my own views, but He put in the mix of all of us His values. He wants you and me to be separate expressions of His love, His compassions, and His mercies. Obviously, this is not something we can do on our own. I'm not even sure I can understand who I am apart from Him. He must do this singular, separate work in each one of us, and then all together we can more accurately look like Him.

As I sat watching our worship team I thought it a good illustration of this. They are supposed to be up on the platform by 7:00 pm and from about 6:30 on, they come up one at a time and begin to play along. Each one adds another dimension to the sound. All are playing the same song, but each one adds its own flavor, and each one builds up the whole. When the group is complete, it becomes a beautiful sound each one reinforcing the others.

We can only find the "my part" in relationship with Him the one who made us to begin with. He has made us the harmony to blend in with the whole team and still play a different part. He is the *Master Conductor,* knowing each one's part, but never playing it for us.

Or again, I can see it in my wife who is uniquely different from who I am, but together we are one. Not only does

He want us to be one with each other, but also He actually wants us to be one with Him. Remember, we are His body.

It's much like the church I attend. We have so many leaders, some on staff and others, like myself who are not, but we are leaders just the same. We are all so different, not one with the same gifting, each one uniquely individual, yet all part of this thing called leadership. So many individually hand crafted gifts, as many as there are faces, and still there will be many more who will have parts to play in days to come. It's as if we are all facets carved into the crown jewel who is Jesus our Lord.

What Have I Learned

_____

_____

_____

_____

_____

_____

_____

_____

_____

_____

_____

_____

_____

_____

_____

_____

_____

_____

_____

_____

_____

_____

_____

6

A Picture of Our Future

W hat did the cross and the pain and suffering on it do for us? Do you remember the story of David and Jonathan and the covenant that they made with each other? After Jonathan and his father, King Saul, had died and David was seated as the King, he remembered the covenant which they had made pertaining to Jonathan's heirs. He found the son of Jonathan and had him brought before the court to fulfill the promise. (II Samuel 9)

In the same way that the king restored everything to the wounded crippled Mephibosheth, who by his own words did not deserve anything but death, likewise you and I also deserve nothing but death. Yet, because of the covenant the King had made many years before, he restored to him all that his family lost and showed Mephibosheth great favor. And now, because of the promises You have given us in Your Word, plus the New Covenant in Your blood, You have restored us into the family of God and given us an inheritance and a relationship which we did not deserve. We know that as faithful as the king was to his friends' son, (because of the covenant), You, Lord, are far more faithful to us, even when we do not deserve it.

The lamb sacrificed on the cross brought about the availability of the restoration of everything we lost in the garden. It's all there. None of it has been lost. It's just been waiting for you and me to know that it belongs to us. The prodigal son did not have to die to be restored. He only had to die to himself and his pride and return to his father's house. This is our story. We've come home to the Father's house and He is waiting to give us the ring, new sandals, and a new robe. This is for the present, not some time in the future. The cross of Christ made it all possible. We now have our new identities, our new righteousness in Christ, and a new foundation. We are the fulfillment all three, the Prodigal son his brother and Mephibosheth!

When John the Baptist saw Jesus coming to where he was baptizing, he made this statement: *"The lamb of God who takes away the sin of the world." (John 1:29)* John the apostle said this about Jesus: *"He is the atoning sacrifice for our sins, and not only for ours but also for the sins of the whole world." (1 John 2:2)*

The penalty for sin has been completely paid for. No works of ours can change this, whether our works are good or bad. You can't be good enough to be saved from the penalty of sin. You can't do works good enough to pay for them. What you can do is say, "Thank you Lord, for Your willingness to pay with Your life, so I could be free from the guilt of my own sin and the sins of my ancestors." You can worship Him and praise Him and tell Him of your love for Him. You can imitate Him in works and in character. You can become a disciple of His and go out into the world and represent Him to all those who don't know Him. But you can't pay the price for sin, no matter how hard you try. It has already been done for you.

What Have I Learned

_____

_____

_____

_____

_____

_____

_____

_____

_____

_____

_____

_____

_____

_____

_____

_____

_____

_____

_____

_____

_____

_____

_____

_____

_____

7
Death; a short study

W hat do we know about death? We know that it is something that all natural living things must go through. It is final and for us there are no negotiations. Once death has occurred you are at the mercy of God.

Now if you understand what the mercy of God means and that you know what the word of God say, then there is no fear of death.

⁹ who has saved us and called us to a holy life— not because of anything we have done but because of his own purpose and grace. This grace was given us in Christ Jesus before the beginning of time, ¹⁰ but it has now been revealed through the appearing of our Saviour, Christ Jesus, who has destroyed death and has brought life and immortality to light through the gospel. 2 Timothy 1:9-10 (New International Version - UK)

God in His mercy brought us the gift of mercy before we ever needed it. Mercy has been ours since before the worlds were formed. Mercy for us has always been on the heart of

God for all of us. He gave it to all He created for He was already aware that we would need it. He made a way, one way for you and I to be restored in righteousness before the fall of man in the garden had even occurred. What an awesome God we serve.

¹ There is a time for everything, and a season for every activity under heaven: ²a time to be born and a time to die, a time to plant and a time to uproot, ³ a time to kill and a time to heal, a time to tear down and a time to build, ⁴ a time to weep and a time to laugh, a time to mourn and a time to dance, ⁵ a time to scatter stones and a time to gather them, a time to embrace and a time to refrain, ⁶ a time to search and a time to give up, a time to keep and a time to throw away, ⁷ a time to tear and a time to mend, a time to be silent and a time to speak, ⁸ a time to love and a time to hate, a time for war and a time for peace. ⁹What does the worker gain from his toil? ¹⁰ I have seen the burden God has laid on men. ¹¹ He has made everything beautiful in its time. He has also set eternity in the hearts of men; yet they cannot fathom what God has done from beginning to end. ¹² I know that there is nothing better for men than to be happy and do good while they live. ¹³ That everyone may eat and drink, and find satisfaction in all his toil— this is the gift of God. ¹⁴ I know that everything God does will endure for ever; nothing can be added to it and nothing taken from it. God does it so that men will revere him. Ecclesiastes 3:1-15 New International Version - UK (NIVUK)

What we know is this; our God has it under control. He knows when, where, what and how things are to be done. They are set in place and we are the only ones who can cut them short or make any change in them. He has made it all available to us but if we want we can do the garden all over again. When we don't take advantage of what God has planned and demand to do it our way, He is no longer responsible for the out come. Then who is, we are! We have judged ourselves unworthy of doing things Gods way.

"I am the Living One; I was dead, and behold I am alive for ever and ever! And I hold the keys of death and Hades." Revelation1:18 New International Version - UK (NIVUK)

Christ Jesus holds the keys of death and Hades. When Jesus went down to hell and took away the key to death He unlocked eternity with that key and there is now no way that death can hold us down. We are immediately in His presence as we see: *"we are of good courage, I say, and prefer rather to be absent from the body and to be at home with the Lord." 2 Corinthians 5:8 New International Version - UK (NIVUK)*

How then can there still be the fear of death either for us or for our loved ones? Is it that we don't know what the word says or are we trapped in unbelief? This is why we call the bible the Good News.

" ²²Men of Israel, listen to this: Jesus of Nazareth was a man accredited by God to you by miracles, wonders and signs, which God did among you through him, as you yourselves know. ²³ This man was handed over to you by God's set purpose and foreknowledge; and you, with the help of wicked men, put him to death by nailing him to the cross. ²⁴ But God raised him from the dead, freeing him from the agony of death, because it was impossible for death to keep its hold on him. ²⁵ David said about him: 'I saw the Lord always before me. Because he is at my right hand, I will not be shaken. ²⁶ Therefore my heart is glad and my tongue rejoices; my body also will live in hope, ²⁷ because you will not abandon me to the grave, nor will you let your Holy One see decay. ²⁸ You have made known to me the paths of life; you will fill me with

*joy in your presence.' ²⁹Brothers, I can tell you confidently that the patriarch David died and was buried, and his tomb is here to this day. ³⁰ But he was a prophet and knew that God had promised him on oath that he would place one of his descendants on his throne. ³¹ Seeing what was ahead, he spoke of the resurrection of the Christ, that he was not abandoned to the grave, nor did his body see decay. ³² God has raised this Jesus to life, and we are all witnesses of the fact."
Acts 2:22-32 New International Version - UK (NIVUK)*

If David could say this and we know that this passage is also messianic scripture then we can all say the same thing about us. The grave cannot hold us.

Baptism is a picture of this in action, only this baptism is for us.

"³ Or don't you know that all of us who were baptised into Christ Jesus were baptised into his death? ⁴ We were therefore buried with him through baptism into death in order that, just as Christ was raised from the dead through the glory of the Father, we too may live a new life ⁵ If we have been united with him like this in his death, we will certainly also be united with him in his resurrection.⁶ For we know that our old self was crucified with him so that the body of sin might be done away with, that we should no longer be slaves to sin—⁷ because anyone who has died has been freed from sin." Romans 6:3-4 New International Version - UK (NIVUK)

What a picture, we are freed from sin and raised up together with Him! I don't think it could be much better and all we have to do is be baptized in the name of Jesus.

¹⁴Since the children have flesh and blood, he too shared in their humanity so that by his death he might destroy him who holds the power of death— that is, the devil— [15] *and free those who all their lives were held in slavery by their fear of death. Hebrews 2:14-15 New International Version - UK (NIVUK)*

Where, O death, is your victory? Where, O death, is your sting? <u>*1 Corinthians 15:55*</u>

Death to our flesh is an opportunity for us to come up higher in our walk with God, death in our physical bodies is an opportunity for us to walk with God again as we did in the garden before we fell. Death is true freedom to be everything we can be. No limitations. But we must not rush this. We have to finish the work He created us to do here first and then only the Father knows when that work is done. Just as the Father only knows when the work of Christ is done in heaven before He sends Him back to gather His bride.

The Cross showed us our worth and the word of God shows us the heart of God to be with us and walk with us. He gave us Himself so this truth could become reality. What an awesome deal.

What Have I Learned

_____

_____

_____

_____

_____

_____

_____

_____

_____

_____

_____

_____

_____

_____

_____

_____

_____

_____

_____

_____

_____

_____

_____

_____

8

Created to be Like Him

There is yet another effect of the cross, or better said, a true benefit from the blood of Christ, that is healing. Some people serve a God who is always changing his mind on many things. Healing is one of them. But it's not for us to believe that He is the never changing God. The Bible says that Jesus went about healing all those who came to Him. This is God the Son or the second part of the God head. He is all God and all man. He represents the goal for you and I. We are being remade according to 2 Corinthians 3:18 into His image as we have already seen. Healing is a large part of that. What Jesus did is what we are called to do.

Remember this statement: *"In the same way I was sent, so I now send you."* In first Peter 2:24 we read: *"by his wounds you have been healed."* This is a quote from Isaiah 53:5, but it has been brought into the present tense exchanging the words "were healed" to "have been healed." Some Bibles use the word stripes, which refers to the beating Jesus took on his back on the way to the cross. We now understand because of this that healing is for today. The church of the New Testament recognized this truth and put it into practice.

"Is any one of you sick? He should call the elders of the church to pray over him and anoint him with oil in the Name of the Lord. And the prayer offered in faith will make the sick person well; the Lord will raise him up. If he has sinned, he will be forgiven. Therefore confess your sins to each other and pray for each other so that you may be healed. The prayer of a righteous man is powerful and effective." (James 5:14-16)

When the Bible says that "by His stripes you were healed", it didn't mean that only those who were present on that day got healed. No, it's for all of us, for all time!

In the book of Hebrews, Chapter 12:12-13, we are told to get our act together so that the sick can be healed. *"Therefore, strengthen your feeble arms and weak knees. Make level paths for your feet, so that the lame may not be disabled, but rather healed."*

So go figure. Why are so many of His creations sick? Someone is not doing his or her jobs. In most cases it's simply because they didn't know it was their job. But it is, and we must be about our Fathers business. Remember, Jesus on that cross said, *"It is finished."* He was announcing to the world that He had accomplished all He had come to earth to do, His job on earth was finished and now it's our turn. He gave us His power and authority to heal the sick and cleanse the lepers.

The point I wish to make very clear is that God's heart for healing has never changed and will never change. It has always been His heart for us to be well. When the children of Israel were brought out of Egypt, which is a picture of you and I being delivered out of our sins, they spent 40 years in good health without sickness. God provided all their needs. God did this and He hasn't changed his mind.

Jesus spent most of his three years of ministry surrounded by sick people wanting to be healed, and guess what, He healed them all!

Have we truly been called to be like Him? Yes! Well, then, let's get to work at it and, please, don't give me that sad story that we have prayed for someone and they didn't get well. That's a copout. Pray for a thousand and let's see how many get healed that wouldn't have if you or someone else didn't pray for them.

Remember this, Jesus told the Canaanite woman that healing was only for the lost sheep of Israel: *"It is not right to take the children's bread and toss it to their dogs."* What we need to see here is that we are now counted with the lost sheep of Israel and that healing belongs to us. We are of the family of God, and, as such, we have every right to the healing power of Jesus. How else would we be able to correctly represent Jesus to the world if we couldn't be like him? But remember this, healing is but one small part of who Jesus is, and so it is with us. There is much more of His image to unfold.

I'm going to pose a question to you that I want you to think very carefully about. How can we imitate God if we are still wearing servant's robes? You are a son as much as Jesus was and, as such, everything that the Father has, has been made available to you. We are all called to serve in one capacity or another, but most of us have not been made aware of the joy of being a son.

Think with me again about the prodigal son. He wanted to come back as a servant but his father would not even hear his argument. The father restored to him his sonship and, as such, he was once again heir to the family inheritance. So are we. The servant's heart as a son comes when we are able to lay aside our royal kingly robes for a time and serve one another. This is what Jesus did when He washed the disciples' feet. He never gave up who He was, but He laid it aside for a moment as an example for us to follow. We are priests and kings as we have been made family. We do not have to apologize for being joint heirs with Christ. It's who we are. Be happy about it and enjoy all the rights and privileges it gives to us.

You, Lord, have bought back for us the right to live in our true identities, to walk in Your kingdom now. We have been given the privilege to be who You made us from the very beginning. We are Adam, made in Your image and likeness.

What Have I Learned

9

The War in Jesus' Garden (Gethsemane)

One last aspect of the work of the cross we have not visited is the gigantic war that was being fought over the life of Christ Jesus just hours before he would die on the tree. And, for that matter, even before His birth when the villagers in Joseph and Mary's hometown wanted to stone Mary who would become the mother of Jesus.

Then, of course, there was King Herod sent his solders to Bethlehem to kill all the babies two years and under to try and make sure Jesus didn't live to be the King. To say He didn't have to die this death would be to say you don't understand that God had to fulfill His work here on Earth and to bring fulfillment to His Word. Remember, the New Testament fulfills the Old Testament and everything has to be brought into full fruition.

My hope is that you can see along with me the magnitude of the love of God for us as the Son of God waged war with His soul this night in the garden on the Mount of Olives. This fight was accomplished by Jesus to overcome the battle we lost with the serpent in the garden of Eden in the beginning.

The agony of the man, His soul, His flesh, and, at the same time, the supernatural Spirit within, encouraging Him, reminding Him what this is all about, helping Him to view the coming hours of great pain and loneliness through His spirit.

I doubt whether any of us have ever sweated blood. The stress of this hour would have broken most of us. Yet I understand that there are those who have been willing to give up their lives for our freedom. But here it is different. God, the Son, would have to give up not only His place in heaven but also the relationship with His Father. We are well acquainted with the story, but what we don't know is the inner battle that was going on for our eternity.

As I sat in His presence during a time of reflection, I ask Him, "Lord, show me the war You fought for my salvation. Show me the battle You had to overcome in Your soul so I could have the freedom of choice to chose to love You or not."

What He showed me was the many times that I have run away from places my spirit wanted to go but my soul refused, and I chose another way. How many wars I have lost to my flesh! I, much like Peter, who within minutes of the time of Jesus' arrest would deny he even knew who Jesus was.

Three times Jesus asked the Father to take this from Him, and also three times He spoke. But, Lord, let Your will be done instead of my soul's. Yes, He could have called the Angels to come and rescue Him, but then He would have to deny the very purpose of His birth and the reason He found himself in the garden on this night. The plan of God was coming to an end.

Oh, the love that made Him stay when He could have just returned to Galilee and the safety of His own town and family. He chose to go to Jerusalem knowing that the cross was waiting for Him there.

He was raised from a baby for this purpose, just as a calf is purposefully raised to be food or a lamb purposefully raised for chops. He knew that He had come as the bread of life to be consumed as a sin offering for those who would believe in Him.

Feel the burden He must have felt as He took on all the sin of the world. He had to carry all this sin to the cross so we could taste freedom. The weight of this sin was crushing the entire world, yet He was faithful to His call. The war was immense, but the battle was won along while all His friends slept. All hail King Jesus, Emanuel!

What Have I Learned

_____

_____

_____

_____

_____

_____

_____

_____

_____

_____

_____

_____

_____

_____

_____

_____

_____

_____

_____

_____

_____

_____

_____

_____

_____

10

This Changes Everything

There is a scripture that, in my opinion, changes every-thing: II Timothy 1:9. This verse tells us that, before time, the secret plan of God was made. Before time broke out of eternity, God had already made a way for us, you and me, to be brought back from the spiritually dead and reunited with Him. This verse makes it all possible: *"⁹Who has saved us and called us to a holy life—not because of anything we have done but because of his own purpose and grace. This grace was given us in Christ Jesus before the beginning of time." (II Timothy 1:9)*

Grace for us was always a part of His plan. The fall of man into sin or the disobedience of Adam and Eve didn't catch God by surprise, for He had already made the provision for our redemption.

Before time (the dimension we live in), God sent His Word into the world to save mankind and to deliver mankind from the consequences of sin. You and I had nothing to do with it! He did it because He loved us and desired to be able to relate once again with His creation. He saw all that would take place from creation to the end and He made a way for us to be with Him.

I hope this little book gives you an understanding of what an awesome creation you are. We are His glory. His righteousness is locked up in us, trying very hard to get out. We are the light that shines in the darkness. Your relationship with Him was always a part of the plan. We are the righteousness of God in Christ Jesus. Sin can't stop us if we don't hold on to it. This is why we can go out in His name and represent Him to the world. It has nothing to do with our good works. He chose all of us to be His body. None were chosen by Him to be left for sin to destroy. That, my friend, is up to you. A simple "yes" to Him and you can be free of the sin that entangles you, free to love and worship your Creator. True freedom is ours and it will always be found in Jesus. (Romans 10:9-11)

Rev. Duane Harlow

What does the cross mean to me? It means love; it means life and that more abundantly. It means living without any fear and knowing that eternity waits for me at the end when my body dies. It means knowing that I get to spend eternity with the one who created me and loved me enough to die for me.

Parting thoughts

*I*f we don't receive these things that are called relationship and restoration, then why did He come? Everything
is about God's unfailing love for His creation. I'm not
talking about all the wonders of this Earth. We, you and I,
are the center of God's love and the target of His grace. He
came to bring restoration to us…How should that make us
feel? Very special indeed! Isn't His Love Truly Amazing!

By Rev. Duane Harlow

Contact Information

Duane Harlow
DuMar Ministries, Inc.
www.DuMarMinistries.com
Dumar888@msn.com

Other Books by
Duane Harlow

Breaking Out of Religious Christianity
Imitate Me

CPSIA information can be obtained at www.ICGtesting.com
Printed in the USA
BVOW021643100712

294826BV00001B/2/P